Bridges

Macdonald Educational

Contents

Did you know?

Forth Railway Bridge, Scotland

House on the Bridge, Ambleside

Bridge of Sighs, Venice

Bridge across the Atlantic

The earliest recorded bridge was built on the Nile by Menes, King of the Egyptians, in about 2650 B.C.

Until recently, some people actually lived in a house on a bridge. You can still see the house, at Ambleside in the English Lake District.

The French acrobat, Jean-Francois Gravelet, who was known as Blondin, made his name by crossing the Niagara Falls on a tightrope bridge, 335 metres long and 50 metres above the water. He repeated this amazing feat several times. He made the crossing on stilts, then he carried a man on his back. Another time he went across in a sack. On yet another crossing, he sat down in the middle to cook and eat an omelette.

The Bridge of Sighs in Venice is so called because it was used as a passageway to lead prisoners from a courtroom to a gloomy gaol.

Since its opening in 1890, the Forth Bridge in Scotland, which some people think is the greatest of all railway bridges, has required constant painting. The red oxide paint which is used keeps the bridge free from rust. As many as 29 men have taken about three years to apply 56 tonnes (45,000 litres) of paint to the 59 hectares of steel tubing. When the painting was complete it was time to start all over again! Since 1976, four men using two small diesel-powered spray guns have replaced the former team of painters and their brushes.

There is even a bridge across the Atlantic Ocean! It joins a small island off the west coast of Scotland to the mainland.

Why Bridges are Built

We do not know who made the first bridge or when it was built. But we can be certain that bridges have been with us for many thousands of years. The Stone Age hunters who roamed the forests in search of food made use of simple bridges. A carefully-placed log could help hunters pursue their prey across a stream that was too deep to wade through or too wide to jump.

The wandering hunters were followed, perhaps 5000 years ago, by the first farmers. Although the farmers settled their homes in one place they still needed to move easily around the countryside. Roads and river crossings were important because the farmers needed to travel from their farmhouses to their fields, and from farm to farm. Trade, and the movement of goods, led to the development of long-distance routes crossing countries and whole continents. Rivers and other obstacles to travellers had to be overcome. Where possible, rivers were crossed at points where the water was shallow enough to allow people and animals to splash through without any danger. But fords, as such crossings are called, cannot be used when a river is in flood. So large stones were sometimes placed at regular intervals across the bed of a river to make the traveller's crossing easier. It was difficult to carry heavy loads across these stones so later, a bridge might be formed by placing blocks of stones or pieces of wood between the stepping stones.

The Bronze Age people of Exmoor constructed a bridge of this type over the River Barr about 3000 years ago. It is still standing, and is known today as the Tarr Steps. 20 piles of large stones were heaped up in the river bed and 24 red sandstone slabs, or clappers, which form the bridge, were laid across them. The Tarr Steps is such a strong bridge that it has survived recent serious floods which have destroyed many more modern structures built of stone and iron.

Many people today travel much further, and much faster, than their ancestors ever did. Bridges are essential to overcome the obstacles that would make our travel difficult and slow. Today they are all around us: bridges to carry roads, railways, canals and pedestrians wherever they want to go.

Above: Tarr Steps Bridge, Exmoor

Right: Fallen tree trunks served as bridges for Stone Age hunters.

Far right: Where rivers were too wide for bridges to be built, ferry boats carried passengers from one bank of the river to another.

Building a Bridge

The simplest kind of bridge is made up of a long piece, or beam, of wood, metal or concrete. The beam is supported at each end by an upright known as a pier. The distance between the piers, the span as bridge-builders call it, cannot be too wide. The prehistoric hunter who placed a wooden log across a stream soon knew if the span was too wide. The hunter's weight, pressing down on the log, would push together the upper layers of the wood. The lower layers would be stretched. At first the log would bend. If the strain of pushing together the top layers and stretching the bottom layers were too great for the log, then it would break. Our hunter might end up in the water! Next time, to stop the log from breaking, the hunter might build supports in the stream, or try to find a stronger log.

Today's bridge-builders deal with the problem in the same way. A long beam bridge is supported on piers built at intervals along its length. This can be very expensive, and when the piers are built in a busy river they can make things difficult for shipping.

Spans are now much greater than they were in the past because engineers have found stronger materials and better ways of using them. Metal is usually stronger than wood, but even steel will break or bend under great pressure. The railway builders of the nineteenth century found that they could increase the strength of a metal beam by adding a framework of jointed pieces of metal. The framework, called a truss, helps to keep the beam firm when it is carrying a load. But if the beam is built in the form of a girder, there is no need for it to be supported by a truss. You can see an example of a girder in the diagram opposite.

Concrete is cheap and easily formed into many shapes. It can be used to make the beam of a bridge. It stands up well to pressure, but it will crack if it is strained too far. Its strength can be increased by reinforcing, or placing steel rods in the bottom of the beam when it is cast. The strength of the concrete can be further increased by stretching the rods before they are placed in the concrete. This is called pre-stressed concrete. Most bridge-builders today use this material because it is strong and safe.

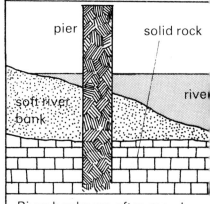

River banks are often marshy. Therefore piers to support bridg may need very deep foundation make them stable.

Building the Medway Bridge in K

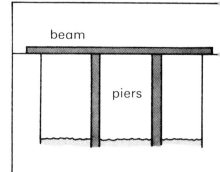

Piers support a simple beam bri to stop it bending and breaking under a heavy load.

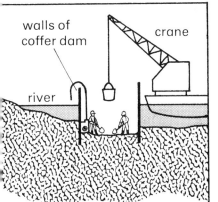

walls of coffer dam

crane

river

igging foundations for a bridge.
he walls of the box-shaped coffer
am hold back the river to allow
ork to go on.

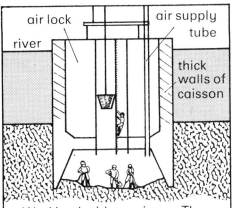

air lock

river

air supply tube

thick walls of caisson

Working inside a caisson. The
sealed chamber allows work to
continue far below the surface of
the water.

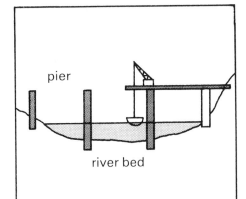

pier

river bed

Building a beam bridge.
Work starts by sinking piers in the
river bed. The roadway is then built
out from the banks.

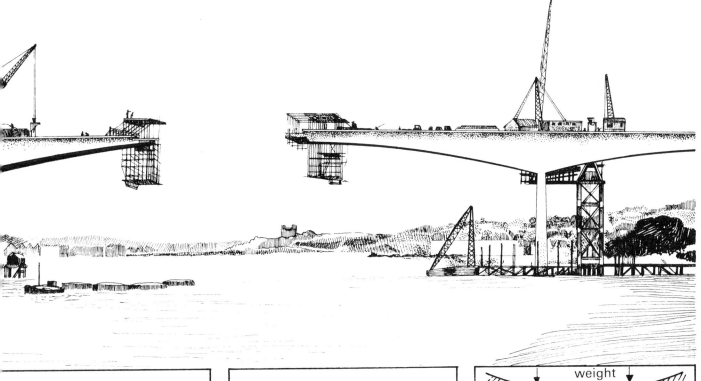

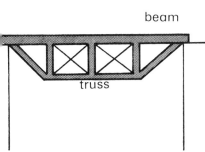

beam

truss

beam bridge can also be
rengthened by a truss, or criss-
oss iron framework. This makes it
ore rigid.

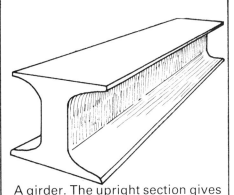

A girder. The upright section gives
strength to the flat surfaces and
prevents them bending or twisting
under pressure.

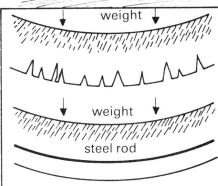

weight

weight

steel rod

Steel rods can be used to
strengthen concrete, which would
otherwise bend and break under a
heavy load.

Landscape with Bridges

There are bridges all around us, over rivers, railways, roads and even over other bridges! There are bridges of all sorts of sizes and shapes. You can make a model landscape to include as many different types of bridges as possible. The landscape shown in the picture here is just an example of the sort of model you could make.

You will need:

paint and paintbrushes

cartridge paper or thin card

scissors

sticky tape

glue

lots of empty cardboard cartons of different shapes and sizes

wool or
string

**To make the base
of your model:**
First, design the layout of your landscape. Mark where the hills, fields and rivers will be. The children in the picture have used a thick sheet of card as a base for their model, and have built hills out of papier mâché, but you could use layers of newspaper or hardboard as a base, and make hills and tunnels out of clay, playdough or Plasticine. Once you have made the base for your model, paint it or stick down sheets of coloured paper to show where rivers, fields and roads are.

**To make the roads,
railways and bridges:**
1. For roads and railways, cut thin strips of black or grey paper and stick them to the base board.

2. To make the bridges, look at the pictures of bridges in books in your nearest library, or in this book, and see what the different types of bridges look like. Try to find out about the following: beam bridges, arch bridges, suspension bridges, cantilever bridges, or just simple log bridges. Now look at the picture of the model bridges on this page and the facing page. How many of these types of bridges can you see? There is, for example, a suspension bridge made out of four toothpaste cartons, some wool and some thin strips of paper. You could make an arch bridge out of two pieces of paper cut out in arch shapes and joined together at the top by a wide strip of paper held in place by sticky tape.

3. When you have made the bridges, you could also make some buildings to go in your landscape. Use cardboard boxes to make blocks of flats, houses, shops or offices. Paint them or stick on doors and windows cut out of coloured paper. Make roofs from folded paper or card. As a final touch, you could add one or two boats to the rivers in your landscape. The picture on the facing page shows a simple boat made out of a cardboard tube and two strips of thick paper.

Single-arch Bridges

The Romans were probably the first to use the arch for bridge building. Arches make strong, safe structures that can even stand up to the weight of present-day traffic. It is possible to bridge wider gaps with an arch than with a simple beam bridge. A stone arch can safely be built with a span of well over 60 metres.

The purpose of an arch is to carry the weight of the bridge and its traffic, or load, safely to the ground. The weight of the bridge and its load is pushing downwards all the time. When it reaches the arch it is turned into an outward force which pushes towards the abutments, the walls on either side of the arch. The abutments have to be strong to withstand these pressures on them.

An arch may be made of wood, metal, stone or concrete. When stone is used, the arch is made up of carefully-cut blocks, known as voussoirs. Round-headed arches were favoured by the Romans. Some bridge builders in the Middle Ages used a pointed arch which is easier to construct. The fact that so many of these arches have survived tells us how strong they are.

In the Middle Ages, bulky goods were carried on horseback. Packhorse bridges were built to make merchants' long journeys from market to market quicker and easier. Most packhorse bridges are built in a single-arch shape. Medieval builders copied the shape from Roman buildings.

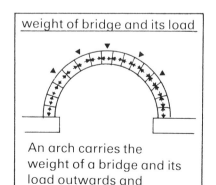

weight of bridge and its load

An arch carries the weight of a bridge and its load outwards and downwards.

The Dog and the Cheese

This is a version of a story first told by Aesop, a Greek story-teller who lived over 2000 years ago. His stories, called fables, were designed not only to entertain his audience, but also to make them think!

Once upon a time, a dog was carrying a cheese he had taken from a nearby farmhouse back to his own home. He was very fond of cheese and held this one tightly between his teeth, for fear of dropping it in the mud. To get home, he had to cross a bridge over a slow and winding stream. Halfway across the bridge, he looked down, and, to his surprise, saw something in the water. At first, he could hardly believe his eyes. It was another dog, carrying another cheese in its mouth!

To be friendly, he wagged his tail. The dog in the water wagged its tail in reply. Very cautiously, he put out a paw to try and touch the other dog. It did the same, straight away. This took him by surprise, and so he growled as best he could through his mouthful of cheese, to warn the other dog not to come too near. It remained silent.

Now, as well as being fond of cheese, he was also a very greedy dog. He began to think how nice it would be to have two cheeses, rather than just one. It seemed that the other dog, who had not replied to his growling, would not put up too much of a fight. So, with a great bound, he leaped at the dog in the water, his mouth wide open to try and snatch the cheese it was holding. Splash! There was a great commotion. Water and mud and weeds flew all around. But the dog in the water was nowhere to be seen. Neither was its cheese. Puzzled, the dog from the bridge looked round for his own cheese, that he had been carrying so carefully all the way home. There it was, at the bottom of the stream. He had dropped it when he jumped into the water to chase his own reflection.

Stepping Stones

Stepping over stepping stones,
 one, two, three,
Stepping over stepping stones,
 come with me!
The river's very fast,
And the river's very wide,
And we'll step across on stepping stones
And reach the other side.

Bryan O'Lynn

Bryan O'Lynn and his wife
 and wife's mother,
They all went over a bridge together;
The bridge broke down,
 and they all tumbled in,
We'll go home by water,
 said Bryan O'Lynn.

Multi-arch Bridges

'I have left a bridge that shall remain forever.' These are the proud words that Caius Julius Lacer had inscribed on his bridge over the River Tagus in Spain. Almost 2000 years later, the 'Puente Trajan', as it is called today, remains as a monument to his skill. The Muslims, who conquered Spain in the 8th century, were so impressed by Lacer's work that they called the place Alcantara – the Bridge – in their own language. Roads and bridges played an essential part in the Roman conquest of Europe. That is why the Emperor Trajan ordered the building of this bridge over the River Tagus, which was a major obstacle to troop movements. The valley was too wide to be spanned by a single arch and so Lacer's bridge rests on seven huge arches.

The roadway over the top of the bridge is 52 metres above the bed of the river. The row of arches rests on massive 9 square metre piers, which rise from the valley floor. They must have been built with great speed, since the River Tagus often floods, and the builder's wooden scaffolding could have been swept away by the rushing floodwaters. The granite blocks from which the bridge was made were cut to shape on the ground and raised into position. Some weigh as much as 8 tonnes. They were lifted 45 metres above the valley floor by a simple crane. They rested on a huge wooden scaffolding until they were all in place. Each block had to fit perfectly against the next one, since no mortar was used. When the final block, the keystone, was positioned, and the arch was complete, each block was held in place by the next. The wooden scaffolding was then taken away.

The Romans knew all there was to know about building single and multi-arch bridges. Their designs have never been bettered. The Puente Trajan was copied by 19th century railway engineers to bridge the River Wear at Lambton in County Durham. Lacer would have been very surprised to see trains speeding over a bridge based on his design! However, the multi-arch bridge, or viaduct, is often the best way of taking a railway over a wide valley. Railway locomotives are unable to climb steep hills, therefore bridges, tunnels and cuttings are used to keep the slope of the track as gentle as possible.

Viaduct Collage

Viaducts are bridges built to carry roads or railways across rough land or river valleys. They are usually built of tiers of arches, one on top of the other, with the road running above the top row of arches.

1. Take the big sheet of white paper. This will form the base of your collage.

2. Take a wide strip of blue paper, and stick it to the base sheet. This will form the river at the bottom of the valley.

3. Take several sheets of brown or grey paper and fold them in half lengthways. Draw semi-circles along the folded edges, as shown. You can use a protractor or compass for this, or trace round the rim of a cup. Cut round the semi-circles.

You will need:

Large sheet of white paper

brown, grey, blue, green paper

glue or sticky tape

scissors

4. Open up one sheet of the paper you have just cut, and stick it down on top of the blue strip, so that the top of the blue is in line with the centre of the circular holes. This sheet forms the bottom row of arches and their reflection in the river.

5. Take the other sheets of brown or grey paper and cut along the folded edges, through the centres of the cut-out circles. Stick them above the first row of arches, to make your viaduct taller.

6. Take a sheet of green paper at least as wide as your base sheet. Fold it in half lengthways and cut out a 'V' shape. Stick it down so that the top of the 'V' is level with the top of your viaduct. This forms the valley.

7. Cut out an engine and some carriages from scraps of coloured paper and stick them on top of your viaduct.

Cold Feet

They have all gone across
They are all turning to see
They are all shouting 'Come on'
They are all waiting for me.

I look through the gaps in the footway
And my heart shrivels with fear,
For way below the river is flowing
So quick and so cold and so clear.

And all that there is between it
And me falling down there is this:
A few wooden planks (not very thick)
And between each, a little abyss.

The holes get right under my sandals,
I can see straight through to the rocks,
And if I don't look, I can feel it
Just there, through my shoes and my socks.

Suppose my feet and my legs withered up
And slipped through the slats like a rug?
Suppose I suddenly went very thin
Like the baby that slid down the plug?

I know that it cannot happen
But suppose that it did, what then?
Would they be able to find me
And take me back home again?

They have all gone across
They are all waiting to see
They are all shouting 'Come on'
But they'll have to carry me.

Brian Lee

Suspension Bridges

Many people think that suspension bridges are the most graceful and spectacular of all bridges. They can be used to span much greater distances than any other type of bridge. In a suspension bridge, the roadway hangs in the air from a pair of cables which rest on two towers, one on or near each bank. Rods called suspenders, or hangers, carry the weight of the roadway and its load up to the cables. The cables are made of thousands of strong wires which are wound tightly together. They carry the weight of the bridge to the towers and down to the anchor points, where they are fixed firmly into the ground.

Bridges made from the rope-like liana plant tied between two trees have been known for centuries. But the suspension bridge as we know it was an invention of the age of iron. In 1820, Captain Samuel Brown suspended a bridge on iron chains over the River Tweed. Six months after it opened, the bridge was blown down.

An American engineer, John Roebling, was convinced that he could build a suspension bridge that would hold firm in the worst of weathers. He used twisted wire cables, instead of chains, and gave extra support by adding a criss-cross network of diagonal braces between the hangers. Roebling's methods remained in use until the 1960s, when new materials enabled engineers to build streamlined road decks to withstand high winds.

In 1867, Roebling was asked to design and construct a bridge across the East River to link Brooklyn with New York. Brooklyn was growing fast and the existing ferry-boat service was unable to meet the demands of the increased traffic. The river was busy too, and nothing could be allowed to get in the path of shipping. The only solution was a huge suspension bridge with a span of 486 metres, nearly half as long again as the longest bridge then existing. Many problems had to be overcome. It was necessary to dig 24 metres below the level of the river bed to find firm foundations on the river's banks in which to build the towers and anchor the cables. Accidents and bad working conditions claimed the lives of 20 men and Roebling himself died from injuries he received at the bridge construction site. The bridge was finally opened in 1887, and now carries 100,000 vehicles a day.

Brooklyn Bridge, USA.

weight of the bridge

anchor point

hangers

cables

tower   tower

river bed

Suspension Bridge at Night

Many bridges are brilliantly lit at night, especially those with tall towers, like suspension bridges. This is so that aircraft can avoid them. Seen from a distance, the lights of a bridge look dramatic and very beautiful against the dark night sky. You can make a string picture of a suspension bridge at night.

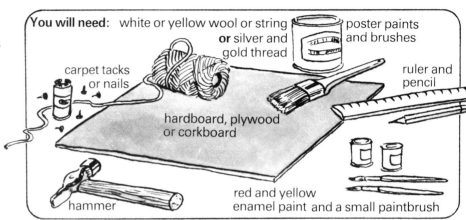

You will need: white or yellow wool or string **or** silver and gold thread — poster paints and brushes — carpet tacks or nails — hardboard, plywood or corkboard — ruler and pencil — hammer — red and yellow enamel paint and a small paintbrush

1. Draw the outline of a suspension bridge on your board. Draw round the edge of a plate, or use compasses, to make the curved top line of the bridge.

2. Mark where to hammer in the nails. Space nails about 3 cm apart.

3. Paint your board black or dark blue. Be careful not to get any dark paint on the heads of the nails. Paint the heads of the nails yellow or red.

4. Now thread your wool or string up and down between the nails. Remember to fasten the end securely when you have finished!

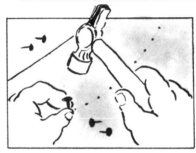

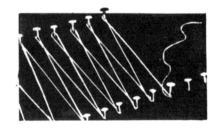

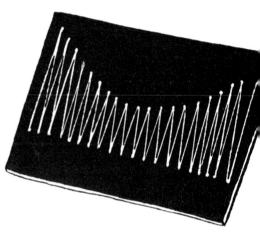

Willow Pattern

Two pigeons flying high
Chinese vessel sailing by,
Weeping willow hanging o'er,
Bridge with three men, if not
    four,
Chinese temple, there it stands,
Seems to cover all the land,
An apple tree with apples on,
A pretty fence to hang my song.

There is a bridge at the centre of the Willow Pattern design which has been used to decorate crockery for almost 200 years. Although the pattern shows a Chinese scene, the design was first made by an English potter.

Willow Pattern was very popular in Victorian times and many stories grew up around the design. One of these is about a young and beautiful Chinese girl, whose name was Koong-Shee.

She was the daughter of a Chinese mandarin, Li-Chi, who lived in a pagoda beneath an apple tree. Li-Chi wanted Koong-Shee to marry an elderly merchant, but she fell in love with her father's secretary, Chang. They met secretly until they were discovered and Chang was sent away. Helped by the mandarin's gardener, who is shown in the design leading them over the bridge, they elope. Li-Chi is angry and follows them with his guard. The lovers are caught and are about to be killed when the gods take pity on them and turn them into a pair of doves.

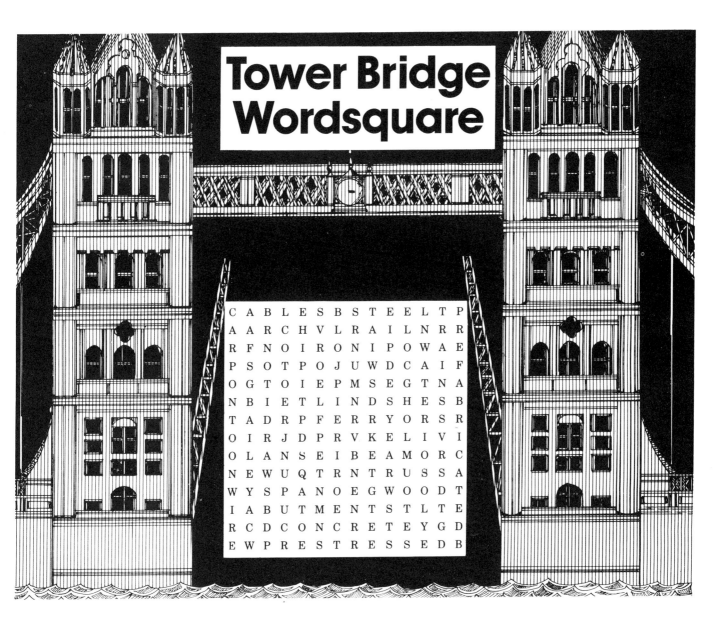

Tower Bridge Wordsquare

```
C A B L E S B S T E E L T P
A A R C H V L R A I L N R R
R F N O I R O N I P O W A E
P S O T P O J U W D C A I F
O G T O I E P M S E G T N A
N B I E T L I N D S H E S B
T A D R P F E R R Y O R S R
O I R J D P R V K E L I V I
O L A N S E I B E A M O R C
N E W U Q T R N T R U S S A
W Y S P A N O E G W O O D T
I A B U T M E N T S T L T E
R C D C O N C R E T E Y G D
E W P R E S T R E S S E D B
```

Hidden in this wordsquare are many of the words connected with bridge-building. Look along the lines, down the lines, and then diagonally, corner to corner, to find them. The following clues will help you in your search. You can find the answers on page 47.

Five materials of which bridges are made.
The piers of a bridge rest on these.
The distance between the piers of a bridge.
A shaped steel plank or plate.
A framework of steel giving added strength to the beam of a bridge.
A way of strengthening concrete.
An aqueduct carries this.
The type of bridge used by pedestrians only.
A bridge made in sections is . . .
A bridge over a castle moat.
A floating bridge.
A temporary bridge built by soldiers.

The Quebec Bridge carries them over the St Lawrence River.
The name of the stones which make up the ring of an arch bridge.
A help to crossing a stream where there is no bridge.
Four types of bridge construction.
It will support a bridge in the middle of a river.
A way of crossing a river where there is no bridge.
The roadway of a suspension bridge hangs from them.
This book is about them!

Cantilever Bridges

The cantilever bridge came into use for bridging wide spans during the great period of railway building in the 19th century. Suspension bridges, as then built, were not thought to be strong enough to carry the weight of rail traffic. A cantilever bridge can carry more weight. It can withstand the pounding of the trains which pass over it, and remains rigid in the strongest winds. Another great advantage of cantilever bridges is that they need no piers to support the weight of the bridge in the middle of the span. They can therefore be built across rivers which have a very fast current, or which are very deep.

A cantilever bridge is made up of two main parts which are the same in every detail. Each main part is made up of a pier and a beam, and usually looks like the letter 'T'. One arm of each is anchored to the bank. It balances the weight of the other arm, the cantilever, which juts out over the river. In most bridges of this type, the two cantilever arms do not meet. Instead, they are joined by a suspended span which is about the same length as each of the cantilever arms.

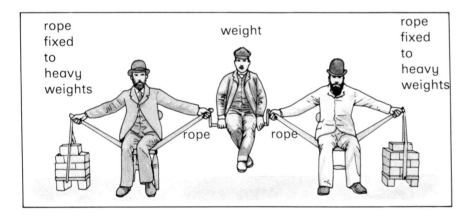

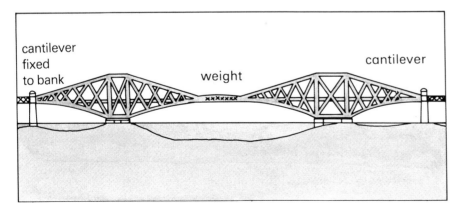

The diagram opposite explains how the cantilevers work. Imagine two people sitting down. Their chairs are too far apart for them to touch hands even when their arms are outstretched. A rope is placed between their outstretched hands. It passes under their chairs to their other hands. The ends of the rope are tied down or weighted. A third person can then sit on the rope between the two seated men. His weight is balanced by the men's outer arms and by the rope which is firmly anchored down.

Although the idea is fairly simple, a cantilever bridge must be carefully designed. Incorrect arithmetic caused the collapse of the first Quebec Bridge. The weight was not evenly spread. Parts of the bridge began to buckle under the stress. In August 1907, the crash came and 9000 tons of steel went down with the men at work on it. A new bridge was built from the foundations of the old. Opened in 1917, the second Quebec Bridge, with a span of 550 metres, carries the railway over the St Lawrence River in Canada.

The Quebec Bridge in Canada carries traffic across the wide St Lawrence river. At the time the bridge was built, the river was used by ocean-going liners with tall funnels. The designers of the bridge had to make sure that the central section, supported by the cantilevers, was high enough to allow these giant ships to pass underneath.

Movable Bridges

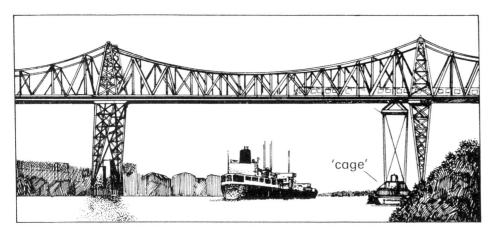

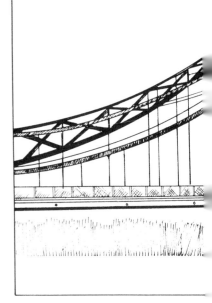

Not all bridges are fixed in one place. When an old bridge is repaired, a temporary structure may be erected in its place. This will usually be made in sections so that it can be put up and taken down again easily. The idea of using bridges built from ready-made parts was first used by army engineers.

An army's success depends on its ability to move people and equipment from one point to another with ease. It may be necessary for troops to cross a river where no bridge exists. A team of engineers goes on ahead and erects a bridge from pre-fabricated sections. When the army has crossed the river, the bridge, known as a Bailey Bridge, will be taken down so that it cannot be used by an enemy. Where a wide river has to be crossed, the bridge might be supported on the decks of flat-bottomed boats called pontoons.

A French engineer, Arnodin, designed another solution to the problem of bridging a river. In his transporter bridge, only a section of roadway is built. You can see a diagram of a transporter bridge above. The

Above:
The Rendsberg Bridge across the Kiel Canal in Germany is a transporter bridge. Cars and trains are carried across the canal in a 'cage' hanging from the bridge.
Below:
Bailey bridges were widely used by the Allied armies during the Second World War. They could be built and taken down again quickly, using ready-made parts.

section of roadway, which looks like a huge metal cage, hangs from girders high above the river. When the cage is loaded with cars it is hauled across the river like an aerial ferry. The Rendsburg Bridge in Germany carries both road and rail traffic over the Kiel Canal.

Other types of bridges have been built with moving parts. Movable bridges helped engineers to overcome one of the most common problems they faced when building bridges. The need to keep shipping lanes open led to the building of high bridges. This was not always possible, and was very expensive. One alternative was to build a low bridge, part of which could be raised to allow ships to sail past.

Tower Bridge across the Thames was completed in 1894. The roadway is in two sections or bascules. Each section is hinged to the bank and can be moved up and down in the same way as a drawbridge. This allows the tallest ships to pass into the Pool of London. Most ships now dock downstream at Tilbury, and Tower Bridge is rarely opened.

The Bridges at Koenigsberg

The town of Koenigsberg stands on the banks of a river in which there are two islands. Seven bridges join these islands to the river banks. In the past, the citizens of Koenigsberg used to take a Sunday afternoon stroll around the town with their families. To amuse themselves, they would try to walk right through the town by crossing all the bridges once only. They found, however, that this just could not be done. To get back to their starting point they had to cross some of the bridges two or more times.

On this page, you can see diagrams of the river and its bridges, and of the route taken by the citizens. The heavy black lines show the paths they took and the black dots show where these paths meet each other. Follow the black lines and see whether *you* can get back to your starting point without retracing your steps.

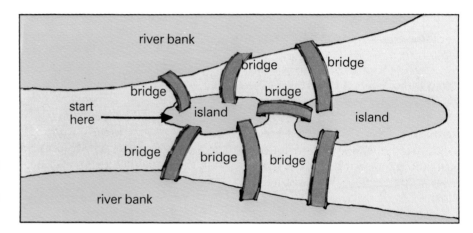

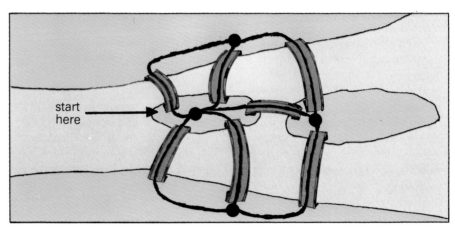

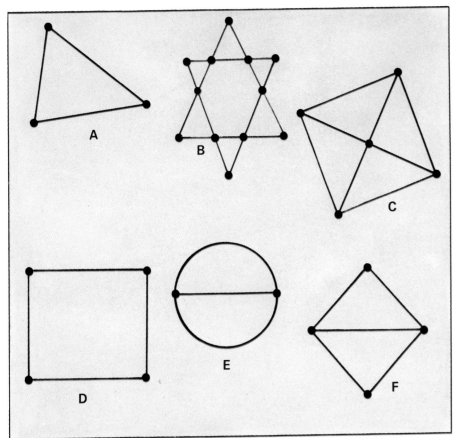

	A	B	C	D	E	F
dots where odd number of lines meet						
dots where even numbers of lines meet	✓					
can be traced without back-tracking	✓					
cannot be traced without back-tracking						
can be traced, but ends at different point from start						

In the 18th century, a famous mathematician called Euler heard about the bridges of Koenigsberg. He also tried, and failed, to get round all of them without retracing his steps. As Euler looked at the map of the Koenigsberg bridges, he began to think. He wondered whether other patterns of pathways were equally difficult to get round without going over some parts of them more than once.

To investigate this, Euler did some experiments by drawing different patterns of lines and dots to represent pathways. He called these patterns 'networks'. As he looked at the networks he had drawn, he made a very surprising discovery. He found that it is possible to predict whether you can get round a network without retracing your steps simply by counting the number of lines which meet at each dot! All you need to do is to decide which of the following three groups your network fits into:

1. Is it a network where an *even* number of lines meet at each dot? If so, you *will* be able to get right round this network without retracing your steps.

2. Is it a network where an *odd* number of lines meet at each dot? If so, you will *not* be able to get round it without retracing your steps **unless**:

3. It is a network where an *odd* number of lines meet at *two dots only* – neither more nor less! You can get round networks like this without retracing your steps, but you will end up at a different point from where you started.

Try these predictions out on the networks in the yellow square. Record your answers in the chart. You should find that networks A, B, D are the first type of network, that network C is the second type, and that E and F are the third!

Now look again at the diagram of the paths across the Koenigsberg bridges. You will see that there are *four* dots where odd numbers of paths meet! What should this tell you?

Euler was very excited by his discoveries of these rules about the way in which pathways around networks behave. You could try to test them further by making drawings of other networks of pathways in your neighbourhood, or perhaps between different parts of your school. Mark in dots for where the pathways meet, and count the number of paths that meet at each dot. Is it an even or an odd number? If an odd number of paths, then are there two dots at which this happens, or more? From these findings, predict whether you will be able to get round the network without retracing your steps. Then check your answer by trying it out. Were you right in your predictions?

Horatius at the Bridge

This is part of a very long – and very famous – poem that was written over 100 years ago. It tells the story of a brave Roman soldier, Horatius. He lived at a time when the Romans were frequently at war with a neighbouring people, the Etruscans. At the start of the poem, Lars Porsena, the Etruscan leader, is planning to attack Rome. The Romans cannot hope to defeat the Etruscans in battle – their only chance of survival is to retreat behind the strong walls of their city. But at one point there are no walls, just a bridge across the River Tiber. The Roman leaders decide to pull down the bridge to try and stop the Etruscan advance. To give them time to do this, Horatius, with two friends, volunteers to guard the approach to the bridge on the **far** bank of the river. Once the bridge has been demolished, they will be alone against the enemy . . .

The poet has used some words which sound a little strange to us today. You can find a list of them on page 2. Poems like this sound splendid when read aloud. Ask an adult to try it and see!

Lars Porsena of Clusium
   By the Nine Gods he swore
That the great house of Tarquin
   Should suffer wrong no more.
By the Nine Gods he swore it
   And named a trysting day,
And bade his messengers ride forth
   East and west and south and north
To summon his array.

★★★

And now hath every city
   Sent up her tale of men;
The foot are fourscore thousand,
   The horse are thousands ten.
Before the gates of Sutrium
   Is met the great array.
A proud man was Lars Porsena
   Upon the trysting day.

★★★

But by the yellow Tiber
   Was tumult and affright:
From all the spacious champaign
   To Rome men took their flight.
A mile around the city
   The throng stopped up the ways;
A fearful sight it was to see
   Through two long nights and days.

★★★

They held a council standing
   Before the River-Gate;
Short time was there, ye well may guess,
   For musing or debate.
Out spake the Consul roundly:
   'The bridge must straight go down;
For since Janiculum is lost,
   Nought else can save the town.'

Just then a scout came flying,
   All wild with haste and fear:
'To arms! To arms! Sir Consul:
   Lars Porsena is here'.
On the low hills to westward
   The Consul fixed his eye,
And saw the swarthy storm of dust
   Rise fast along the sky.

And nearer fast and nearer
   Doth the red whirlwind come;
And louder still and still more loud,
   From underneath that rolling cloud
Is heard the trumpet's war-note proud,
   The trampling and the hum.
And plainly and more plainly
   Now through the gloom appears,
Far to the left and far to right
   In broken gleams of dark blue light
The long array of spears.

But the Consul's brow was sad,
   And the Consul's speech was low,
And darkly looked he at the wall,
   And darkly at the foe.
'Their van will be upon us
   Before the bridge goes down;
And if they once may win the bridge,
   What hope to save the town?'

★★★

Then out spoke brave Horatius
   The Captain of the gate:
'To every man upon this earth
   Death cometh soon or late;
And how can man die better
   Than facing fearful odds,
For the ashes of his fathers
   And the temples of his Gods?'

'Hew down the bridge, Sir Consul,
   With all the speed ye may;
I, with two more to help me,
   Will hold the foe in play.
In yon strait path a thousand
   May well be stopped by three.
Now who will stand on either hand
   And keep the bridge with me?'

Then out spoke Spurius Latius
   A Ramnian proud was he:
'Lo, I will stand at thy right hand,
   And keep the bridge with thee.'
And out spake strong Herminius,
   Of Titian blood was he:
'I will abide on thy left side,
   And keep the bridge with thee.'

'Horatius', quoth the Consul,
   'As thou sayest, so let it be.'
And straight against that great array
   Forth went the dauntless Three.

★★★

Now while the Three were tightening
   Their harness on their backs,
The Consul was the foremost man
   To take in hand an axe:
And Fathers mixed with Commons
   Seized hatchet, bar and crow,
And smote upon the planks above,
   And loosed the props below.

Meanwhile the Tuscan army
   Right glorious to behold,
Came flashing back, the noonday light,
   Rank behind rank, like surges bright
Of a broad sea of gold.
   Four hundred trumpet sounded
A peal of warlike glee,
   As that great host, with measured tread,
And spears advanced, and ensigns spread,
   Rolled slowly towards the bridge's head,
Where stood the dauntless Three.

★★★

But all Etruria's noblest
   Felt their hearts sink to see
On the earth the bloody corpses
   In the path of the dauntless Three:
        ★★★

Was none who would be foremost
   To lead such dire attack;
But those behind cried 'Forward!'
   And those before cried 'Back!'
And backward now and forward
   Wavers the deep array:
And on the tossing sea of steel,
   To and fro the standards reel;
And the victorious trumpet peal
   Dies fitfully away.
        ★★★

But meanwhile axe and lever
   Have manfully been plied;
And now the bridge hangs tottering
   Above the boiling tide.
'Come back, come back, Horatius!'
   Loud cried the Fathers all.
'Back Lartius! back Herminius!
   Back ere the ruin fall!'

Back darted Spurius Lartius;
   Herminius darted back;
And, as they passed, beneath their feet,
   They felt the timbers crack.
But, when they turned their faces,
   And on the farther shore
Saw brave Horatius stand alone,
   They would have crossed once more.
        ★★★

But with a crash like thunder
   Fell every loosened beam,
And, like a dam, the mighty wreck
   Lay right athwart the stream:
And, like a horse unbroken,
   When first he feels the rein,
The furious river struggled hard
   And tossed his tawny mane
And burst the curb, and bounded
   Rejoicing to be free,
And whirling down, in fierce career,
   Battlement, and plank and pier,
Rushed headlong to the sea.
        ★★★

Alone stood brave Horatius,
   But constant still in mind;
Thrice thirty thousand foes before
   And the broad flood behind.
        ★★★

But he saw on Palatinus
   The white porch of his home
And spake to the noble river
   That rolls by the towers of Rome.

'O Tiber! father Tiber!
   To whom the Romans pray,
A Roman's life, a Roman's arms
   Take thou in charge this day!'
So he spake, and speaking sheathed
   The good sword by his side,
And with his harness on his back
   Plunged headlong in the tide.

But fiercely ran the current,
   Swollen high by months of rain;
And fast his blood was flowing
   And he was sore in pain.
And heavy with his armour
   And spent with changing blows;
And oft they thought him sinking
   But still again he rose.

'Curse on him!' quoth false Sextus,
   'Will not the villain drown?
But for this stay, ere close of day
   We should have sacked the town!'
'Heaven help him!' quoth Lars Porsena,
   'And bring him safe to shore;
For such a gallant feat of arms
   Was never seen before'.

And now he feels the bottom
   Now on dry earth he stands;
Now round him throng the Fathers
   To press his gory hands;

And now with shouts and clapping,
   And noise of weeping loud,
He enters through the River-Gate,
   Borne by the joyous crowd.
        ★★★

And they made a molten image
   And set it up on high,
And there it stands unto this day
   To witness if I lie.
        ★★★

And underneath is written
   In letters all of gold,
How valiantly he kept the bridge
   In the brave days of old.

A Bridge in History

London is where it is because of the River Thames. The tidal river provided a safe anchorage for seafaring vessels. Small boats carrying many different cargoes could sail up the river into the heart of England. The city itself grew up around the first possible bridging point upstream from the sea.

There has been a succession of bridges at the same point on the river from Roman times. The city was built on the higher ground of the north bank, which was well drained and easily defended. The dry ground on the opposite bank allowed for the meeting of roads. The first bridges were built of wood. One was destroyed by the Vikings. Another was completely swept away during a violent storm. A third was burnt down.

The first stone bridge was begun in 1176 under the direction of a priest, Peter of Colechurch. The roadway, 282 metres long, was built on 19 pointed arches. One section of the roadway could be raised like a drawbridge to allow larger vessels to navigate the river. This drawbridge, together with gate-towers on the north and south banks, served to defend the bridge and the city against attack. The heads of traitors placed on spikes above the gates were a grim warning to would-be rebels. Building the bridge across a busy river proved a difficult task. Each of the massive piers took 19 months to build, and involved the damming up of sections of the river. The work took 33 years to complete. But it was worth the time and trouble: Peter of Colechurch's bridge lasted for over 600 years! Sadly he did not live to see his work finished and was buried in the chapel on the bridge.

For 600 years, Old London Bridge bustled with life. Shops and houses were built along its whole length. The bridge was the site of many pageants and ceremonies. It also served as a grandstand from which Londoners could view processions of barges, water sports and even frost fairs held on the frozen Thames. But an increase in shipping, and rebuilding work which made the channels between the piers very narrow, made Old London Bridge a hazard. And the pressure of water flowing through the narrow gaps between the piers damaged the bridge. It was pulled down in 1833 and has been rebuilt twice since.

Old London Bridge. This picture is copied from a drawing made in the 17th century. You can see the tall houses and shops crowded on the bridge, and in the background to the left, the heads of executed criminals displayed on long poles!

Key

site of city of London

London Bridge

marsh

roads

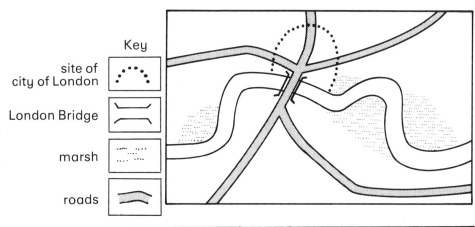

London Bridge

London Bridge is falling down,
Falling down, falling down,
London Bridge is falling down
My fair lady!

How shall we build it up again,
Up again, up again?
How shall we build it up again
My fair lady?

Build it up with silver and gold,
Silver and gold, silver and gold,
Build it up with silver and gold
My fair lady!

Silver and gold will be stolen away,
Stolen away, stolen away,
Silver and gold will be stolen away
My fair lady!

Build it up with iron and steel,
Iron and steel, iron and steel,
Build it up with iron and steel
My fair lady!

Iron and steel will bend and bow,
Bend and bow, bend and bow,
Iron and steel will bend and bow
My fair lady!

Build it up with wood and clay,
Wood and clay, wood and clay,
Build it up with wood and clay
My fair lady!

Wood and clay will wash away,
Wash away, wash away,
Wood and clay will wash away
My fair lady!

Build it up with stone so strong,
Stone so strong, stone so strong,
Then it will last for ages long
My fair lady!

Oh, but London Bridge is falling down,
Falling down, falling down,
London Bridge is falling down
My fair lady!

Traditional nursery rhyme

17th Century Londoners

London Bridge in the 17th century would have been crowded with people visiting the shops on the bridge, hurrying home or stopping to gaze at ships and barges on the River Thames. There would also have been beggars asking for charity, children waiting to run errands as well as thieves and pickpockets.

Imagine that you are a 17th century Londoner. Perhaps you are a rich merchant's wife, going to see what new jewels are for sale in one of the expensive shops. Or perhaps you are a student, visiting one of the new bookshops on the bridge. Perhaps you are a pickpocket, or a fruitseller numb with cold after a long day spent near the water. You could even be a builder, at work on repairs to the bridge. How would you feel about Old London Bridge?

Why not dress up and act out these parts – or imagine other people who might be crossing the bridge at some time in its history.

For a 17th century costume, you will need:

1. A square of material, perhaps an old scarf or a tea-towel. This will make an apron or a sash.

2. Some white paper. Fold this into pleats and then thread some cotton through it using a thick needle to make a ruff.

3. Some squares of cardboard, covered with silver foil or painted silver. Fix elastic bands to these to make buckles for your shoes.

4. A paper doily. Fasten this to your head with hairgrips to make a lace cap.

5. If you decide to play the part of a pedlar, you could make a tray out of a shoe-box lid, and fill it with a selection of goods for sale.

Race to the Castle

You live in a little cottage in the woods. One day, you overhear some outlaws plotting to attack the castle where a lonely princess lives. If you can get a warning to her guards they will prepare the castle to withstand an attack. If you cannot reach the castle in time, the outlaws will make a surprise attack and kidnap the princess.

You and some friends decide to try to get a message to the castle as quickly as you can. To reach the castle, you have to cross a winding stream. You have a choice of two paths to follow. If you take the upper path, you can cross the stream by a strong bridge or by stepping stones, but you may meet with many delays. If you take the lower path, you should meet with fewer accidents to delay you, but you may have to wait for a broken bridge to be mended at the start of your journey.

Play this game with one or more friends. You will need a dice, and a different-coloured counter for each player. Choose which path you want to follow. Then throw the dice and see how many moves to make along the pathway. If you land on a space with instructions to 'stop' or 'wait' on it, miss one turn. If you land on the broken bridge on the lower pathway, wait until you have thrown a '6' before you start to move again. See who is first to reach the castle with the urgent warning!

stop! help gather the harvest

stop! go huntin

stop! pigs on the road

stop! buy apples

stop! fight a duel

stop! play with friendly dog

START 1

stop! argue with fruit-seller

stop! wave goodbye to your mother

wait to throw 'six' while bridge is repaired

stop! help mother and baby

START 2

Bridge Disasters

The night was dark and cold. It had been raining since mid-afternoon. The storm was now at its height. A strong gust of wind almost blew away the baton which the signalman handed to the train driver. In his diary, against the entry for 28th December, 1879, the signalman wrote, '7.15 p.m. Edinburgh Mail train'. The train moved out slowly on to the single track bridge over the estuary of the River Tay. The train was already late. On the north bank of the river, a group of people had gathered to see it arrive. They could hear nothing over the howling of the gale. Then, in the blackness before them, they saw a flash of sparks and a trail of light sweeping down into the swirling waters of the Tay. Two brave men crawled out along the track to see what had happened. The tragedy of that night became clear when they reached a point where the bridge disappeared. The high span of the bridge, almost a kilometre long, had blown down with the train on it. There were no survivors. At least 75 people had lost their lives on that dreadful night.

The country was shocked. Queen Victoria had opened the Tay Bridge less than two years earlier. Newspapers had called it a triumph of modern engineering. People wanted to know what had caused the bridge to collapse. An enquiry found that when the train was in the high girders of the bridge, it presented a solid wall to the wind. The winds, blowing at up to 160 kilometres per hour, struck the large exposed surface area with full force. The bridge and the train were swept away, like a piece of paper blown by the wind.

Many factors can cause a bridge to collapse. The diagrams opposite show some of the most common reasons for bridge failure.

The Tay Bridge disaster and the collapse of other bridges have taught bridge builders a great deal. Before a bridge is begun, engineers carefully work out how the structure will behave in the worst conditions. A scale model might be built and tested in a tunnel through which air is blown. The materials and construction are checked at every stage of building. Every possible care is taken to reduce the risk of disaster.

This picture of the Tay Bridge Disaster appeared in a newspaper shortly after the tragedy happened. It shows rescuers braving rough seas to search for survivors.

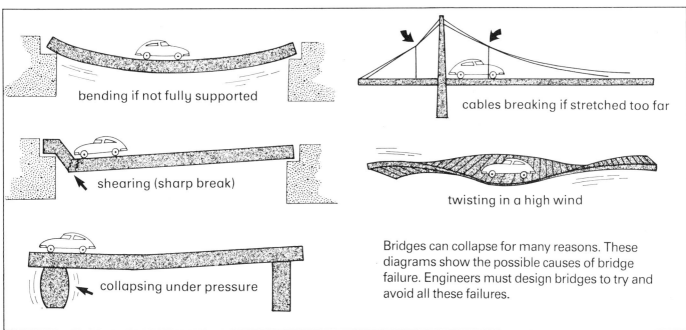

bending if not fully supported

cables breaking if stretched too far

shearing (sharp break)

twisting in a high wind

collapsing under pressure

Bridges can collapse for many reasons. These diagrams show the possible causes of bridge failure. Engineers must design bridges to try and avoid all these failures.

The Best Shape for a Bridge

A bridge must be strong, to withstand the weight of traffic that passes across it. These experiments will help you to find out which is the strongest shape to use for building a simple bridge.

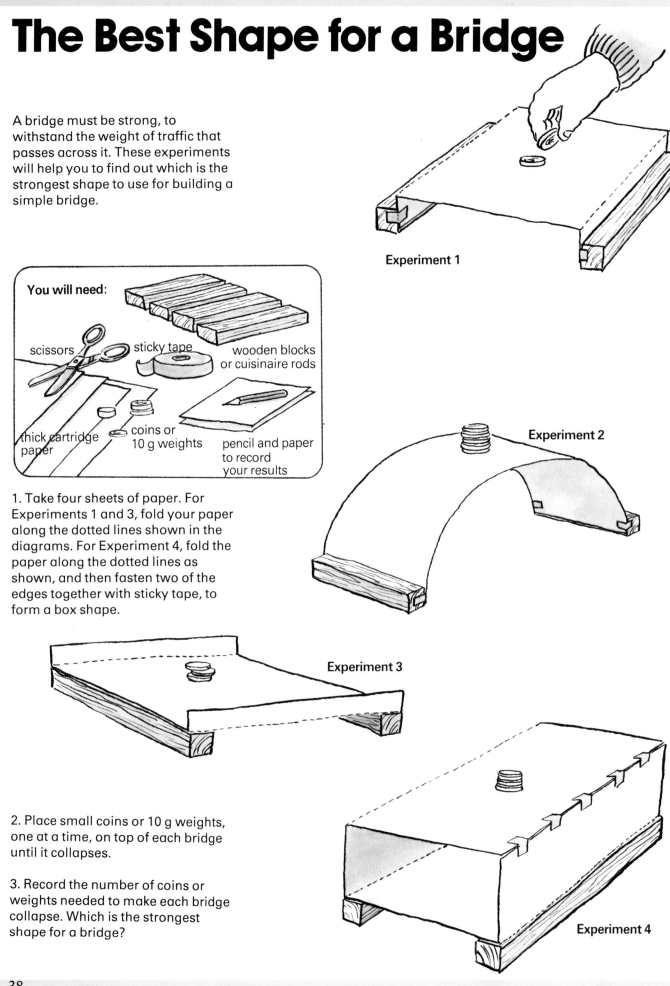

Experiment 1

You will need:

scissors, sticky tape, wooden blocks or cuisinaire rods, thick cartridge paper, coins or 10 g weights, pencil and paper to record your results

1. Take four sheets of paper. For Experiments 1 and 3, fold your paper along the dotted lines shown in the diagrams. For Experiment 4, fold the paper along the dotted lines as shown, and then fasten two of the edges together with sticky tape, to form a box shape.

Experiment 2

Experiment 3

2. Place small coins or 10 g weights, one at a time, on top of each bridge until it collapses.

3. Record the number of coins or weights needed to make each bridge collapse. Which is the strongest shape for a bridge?

Experiment 4

Test the Strength of Bridges

Experiment 1

1. Using the paper fasteners, join the cardboard or plastic strips together to make a variety of shapes. You may need to use the hole punch to make holes at each end.

2. Try gently pulling the shapes you have made. You will find that some of them can easily be pulled out of shape. Which ones cannot be pulled out of shape?

You will need: needle and thread
paper fasteners
a hole-punch
matchbox tray
sticky tape
coins or 10 g weights
strips of cardboard or plastic

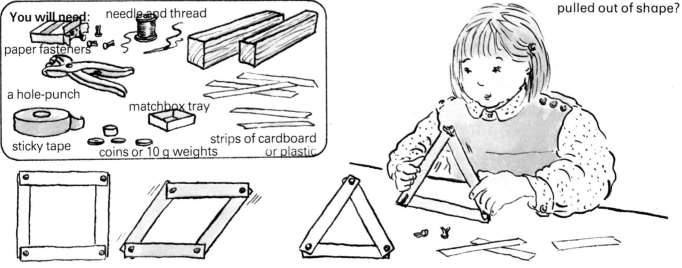

3. You should find that frameworks made of triangular shapes, or of shapes that can be divided into triangles, cannot be pulled out of shape. They are the most rigid.

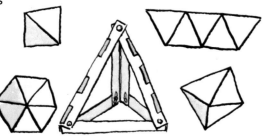

Experiment 2

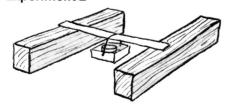

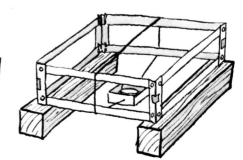

1. Using cardboard or plastic strips, and paper fasteners where necessary, build 4 bridges, as shown in the diagrams. Bridges 1 and 2 are made by simply resting one or two strips across two wooden blocks. For Bridge 3, make a box-shaped framework. For Bridge 4, make a framework composed of triangles.

2. Test which is the strongest bridge by hanging coins or weights from each bridge. Which bridge will support the greatest weight?

3. You should find that the bridge made of triangular shapes is the strongest.

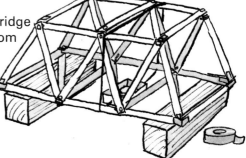

Rainbow Bridges

Many people have believed that rainbows are more than just beautiful shapes in the sky. Some, like Noah at the end of his adventures in the Ark, saw a rainbow as a message from God. Others, like the Scandinavian tribes who lived in Northern Europe over a thousand years ago, thought that the rainbow was a bridge between the earth and the kingdom of their gods. They called the kingdom Asgard, and the rainbow bridge Bifrost. They described the bridge Bifrost as being made of air and water, and always glowing with fire. It was very strong, and more skilfully constructed than any bridge on earth. At the end of this mighty bridge, the gateway to Asgard was guarded by one of the gods themselves. His name was Heimdall. He was always alert and watchful. Because he was a god he needed no sleep and could see by day and by night. In his hand he held a great hunting horn, which he would blow to summon help if ever the rainbow bridge was attacked.

Scandinavian poets told wonderful stories about the rainbow bridge. It was strong enough, they said, to survive any attack except for the final battle which would herald the end of the world itself. Then, the giants who lived in a terrible country of fire and ice called Muspel would rise up to fight the gods, and would break down the beautiful rainbow bridge in their attempt to get across it to Asgard. By the end of this dreadful battle, the whole world would be destroyed. But straight away a new Asgard and a new earth would be born out of the ruins of the old, and a new rainbow bridge would stand shining in the sky to restore the link between them.

Here is part of a poem by the 19th century poet, Christina Rosetti, also about rainbow bridges:

> There are bridges on the rivers,
> As pretty as you please;
> But the bow that bridges heaven,
> And overtops the trees,
> And builds a road from earth to sky,
> Is prettier far than these.

Bridges All Around Us

It is difficult to imagine London without Tower Bridge, Sydney without the Harbour Bridge or San Francisco without the Golden Gate Bridge. These bridges are a vital part of the great cities to which they belong. Tourists visit them and take photographs in the same way that they would a castle, a palace or a church. Many bridges are looked upon as impressive buildings or monuments in their own right.

Bridges are among the biggest things that people have made. Our eyes may be drawn to them because of their sheer size. But it is not only the big or monumental bridges that attract our attention in town and countryside. Bridge building has increased with the growth of traffic. Now there are bridges all around us. We see them everyday.

A bridge in its setting can make a pleasing picture. Bridges have provided a popular subject for artists. In the parks which surround some large country houses, there are sometimes bridges without any real purpose. They were built to please the eye and enrich the view.

The ornamental bridge at Kenwood, London. It was built during the 18th century to improve the view across the lake and has no real usefulness to travellers at all!

'Spaghetti Junction', near Birmingham. Here, roads linking several major motorways cross and re-cross each other, making a complete landscape in themselves.

But not all bridges fit so well into their surroundings. Some modern motorway bridges seem to take over the whole landscape, or so some people say. Do you agree? Because they carry a constant flow of traffic, including huge lorries with heavy loads, these motorway bridges have to be large and strong. Whole sections of the roadway are sometimes carried above ground level on bridges known as flyovers, or beneath other roads in tunnels called underpasses.

Many writers have described not only the best way to build bridges, but also the way they should look. Vitruvius, the famous Roman architect, said that a good bridge should be both strong and sturdy and attractive to look at. But people's views as to what is beautiful differ a great deal. All around, you can see many different types of bridges. Some are plain and simple, others are elaborately decorated. But all have been designed by somebody to look the way they are. See how many different designs for bridges you can spot on the next long journey you make. Which designs do you like best?

The Mouse-deer and the Crocodile

In the hot and steamy forests of Malaya lived a creature known as a mouse-deer. She was called a mouse-deer because she was the very smallest type of deer. But, despite her size, she was brave and clever and cunning, and well able to look after herself.

One day, she set off to visit some relations. The path to the forest where they lived led across a wide river. But when the mouse-deer came to the river bank, she found that the bridge had been washed away by floodwaters. She sat down to think about what she should do next.

While she was sitting there, looking across at the far bank, a crocodile swam up to her. He was hungry and would have liked nothing more than a mouse-deer for breakfast. But he pretended to be friendly. 'Hello,' he said, 'and how are you today?'

'Very cross,' the mouse-deer replied. 'I was on my way to visit my relations but, as you can see, the bridge has been swept away.'

'So it has,' sneered the crocodile, forgetting for a moment that he was trying to be friendly, 'What a pity.'

The mouse-deer ignored him and, after a few minutes' pause, said thoughtfully, 'Is it true that your family isn't doing too well? I hear that many of your relations have fallen sick and died, and that others have left the river.' She went on, 'I come from a very large family myself, you know. We mouse-deer are well-known and respected in these parts.' The crocodile was furious. He splashed about in the water and beat his tail from side to side. 'Who has been telling you lies about my family?' he snarled. 'We are all very well. Never better, in fact. And I bet that my family is bigger than yours. Why, I have 328 aunts and 516 cousins, and I have lost count of some of the more distant branches of my family. If you don't believe me, I will call them all here for you to see for yourself.'

'Oh, please do, crocodile,' said the mouse-deer. 'Then I can tell everybody that your family is not fading away, after all.'

So the crocodile shouted and called, and the mouse-deer watched and waited. She took care to stand just out of the crocodile's reach on the river bank, to be on the safe side. He might get even hungrier while he was waiting for his relations to arrive.

In a very short while, the river was full to the brim of crocodiles. They splashed and snapped and laughed and talked. It was a grand family reunion. The sight of so many fierce creatures would have frightened many other animals, but the mouse-deer was not afraid. 'You were right after all,' she said to the crocodile. 'I'm sorry that I ever believed those lies they told in the forest about your family. Just to check, though, I'd like to count some of your relations for myself. How many aunts did you say you had?'

'328', said the crocodile proudly. 'You can see them over there.' And he waved one of his front legs towards a solid line of crocodiles, all gossiping and chattering away to each other.

'There are so many of them,' said the mouse-deer, 'that I can hardly see the other side of the river. If I'm going to count them, I shall have to get closer to them, so as not to mix them up.' Then she smiled. 'I've got an idea,' she said. 'Would they mind if I climbed on their backs to count the ones that are furthest away?'

'Not if I ask them nicely,' said the crocodile. 'And I'll make them stay still, too. We wouldn't want you falling into the water while you're busy counting my family.' He was so proud of his family that he really meant this, and said it without his usual nasty grin.

So he called to the seething mass of crocodiles. It took some time to quieten them down, but eventually they were all so still that they looked just like a huge raft of logs floating in the water.

This was exactly what the mouse-deer had planned. Counting loudly, she hopped from one crocodile to another, until, by the time she had counted up to 327 she had reached the bank on the other side of the river. With a sigh of relief, she leaped on to the dry land. 'Thank you very much, crocodiles,' she called as she ran off into the forest, 'for making a replacement bridge for me!'

Voices

I heard those voices today again:
Voices of women and children, down in that hollow
Of blazing light into which swoops the tree-darkened lane
Before it mounts up into the shadow again.

I turned the bend – just as always before
There was no one at all down there in the sunlit hollow;
Only ferns in the wall, foxgloves by the hanging door
Of that blind old desolate cottage. And just as before

I noticed the leaping glitter of light
Where the stream runs under the lane; in that mine-dark archway
— Water and stones unseen as though in the gloom of night –
Like glittering fish slithers and leaps the light.

I waited long at the bend of the lane,
But heard only the murmuring water under the archway,
Yet I tell you, I've been to that place again and again,
And always, in summer weather, those voices are plain,
Down near that broken house, just where the tree-darkened lane
Swoops into the hollow of light before mounting to shadow again.

Frances Bellerby

A Bridge for the Future

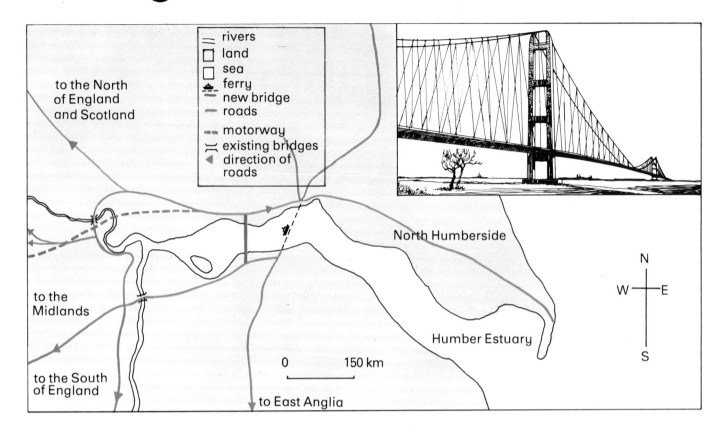

The bridge was probably the first piece of engineering ever attempted. Its invention was second only to that of the wheel in making it easy for people to move around freely. Over the years, the demand for bridges has grown. Bridge-builders are called upon to bridge wider and wider spans. Their powers have been stretched to find safe ways of crossing wider gaps. New ways of using iron, steel and concrete have been found to meet these demands. The success of the bridge-builders' designs has also helped to bring about changes in the way in which other buildings, especially tall blocks of offices and flats, are planned and constructed.

The most recent bridges have been designed with the help of computers and tested in wind tunnels. Many of the latest ideas in bridge building have come from people working on the design of aircraft. The bridges of today, like aeroplanes, are shaped so that the wind does not affect their operation. They have the same streamlined shapes. Some people think they look very elegant, although others prefer older bridges to look at. A new bridge can also be exciting. Its shape looks to the future and suggests what tomorrow's world may look like.

The new Humber suspension bridge is one of the most ambitious engineering projects of recent years. The bridge links the industrial area of North Humberside with the rest of England. Before the bridge was built, travellers had either to make a long journey round the Humber Estuary, or else use the old ferry, which was unsuitable for modern heavy lorries.